# In the Days of
# the Cotton Wind
# and the Sparrow

"Rafi Aaron's poems bask in the ethos of a world of prophets on mountaintops, and stray-travellers-at-your-door, timeless and existing in different incarnations. Everywhere there is the whisper of a teasing seductress, fraught with confusion, sackcloth and uncertainty, and in that whisper you hear the master of the poet's craft, banishing your thirst for travel beyond the borders of all that you know."

—PAUL HAMANN, *The New Quarterly*

His prose poems are "powerful, evocatively imagined works, rich in detail, and intellectual resonance."

—*The Malahat Review*

Rafi Aaron is a poet "who allows simple, fresh, vivid words to cut individual jewels out of the material of language."

—*Toronto Star*

# IN THE DAYS OF
# THE COTTON WIND
# AND THE SPARROW

## Rafi Aaron

Edited by
## Jeff Bien

Publishers of Singular
Fiction, Poetry, Nonfiction, Translations and Drama

Library and Archives Canada Cataloguing in Publication

Aaron, Rafi, author
In the days of the cotton wind and the sparrow / Rafi Aaron ;
edited by Jeff Bien.

Poems.
Issued in print and electronic formats.
ISBN 978-1-55096-658-9 (softcover).--ISBN 978-1-55096-659-6 (EPUB).--
ISBN 978-1-55096-660-2 (MOBI).--ISBN 978-1-55096-661-9 (PDF)

I. Title.

PS8551.A76I58 2017        C811'.54        C2016-907517-6
                                          C2016-907518-4

Copyright © Rafi Aaron, 2017
Design and composition by Michael Callaghan
Edited by Jeff Bien
Cover photograph by Alfredo Ruiz Huerga
Author photograph by Ruth Kaplan
Typeset in Bembo at Moons of Jupiter Studios

Published by Exile Editions Limited ~ www.ExileEditions.com
144483 Southgate Road 14, Holstein, Ontario, N0G 2A0
Printed and Bound in Canada by Marquis

We gratefully acknowledge the Canada Council for the Arts,
the Government of Canada, the Ontario Arts Council,
and the Ontario Media Development Corporation
for their support toward our publishing activities.

 Conseil des Arts du Canada   Canada Council for the Arts

Canadian sales representation:
The Canadian Manda Group, 664 Annette Street,
Toronto ON  M6S 2C8   www.mandagroup.com    416 516 0911

North American and international distribution, and U.S. sales:
Independent Publishers Group, 814 North Franklin Street,
Chicago IL  60610    www.ipgbook.com    toll free: 1 800 888 4741

*For Natacha*
*You brought new colours to my life*
*and woke the eye of the sun in the darkest of hours*

Contents

*To dream is to reconfigure the stars with your left hand*
*while the right conducts four minstrels*
*who have left their instruments in some forgotten place.*

R. A.

# By the Late Night Fire

They told our stories by the late night fire. And we
watched the silent movements that slowed the
onslaught of words: the way an image was
summoned to the mouth or the streams where the
real and imaginary mingled, and where a
trembling finger touches only you.

And we wondered who or what would appear; the
muted thunder calling the rain back to a forgiving
cloud, the leaves of abandoned trees, you and your
beloved and all of summer alive and breathing.

The wind was humming, the clouds shifted, the
chariots of a god barely visible, the nymph
holding the reins and the riding crop high, while
the glazed eye of the moon looked over an empty
battlefield.

Then the long sleeve of the storyteller falling over
his arm, covering our future in sackcloth and
uncertainty. With a walrus's tooth he ripped
words open. The tale had begun, the slaying of
truth, echoes surrounding us, and laughter stood,
motionless, in the valley.

## The Hunting Party

I remember how rivers swelled and the blood
flowed from a red tourniquet tied tight around the
pale white sky. Soon the hunters would head into
the forest. These were nights of sleeplessness, the
wild boar, and the one long tooth of the tiger
devouring dreams. These were also the nights of
forgiving love, where a woman braided years of
passion into a keepsake that waved like wild grass
at the entrance of the heart. The feast began. The
fires were lit to the eye of the Watchful One who
would lead the weary home. No one ate well. Our
thoughts were in the deepest part of the forest, that
place where tall vines strangle the uncharted years
and the husk of a single word wounds the tongue.
Yes, death was calling, it was the same dark sound
we knew but never named, the same silence night
plunges into the back of the retreating light.

# They Disappeared in the Night

They disappeared in the night as the white ash of
the fire went cold. They disappeared with the tales
the almond tree had overheard. Only the stray
mountain goat and the restless stones that
wandered with our people for years knew their
story.

You must understand they left us the way a leper
leaves you living in the weak house of your skin.
It was late in the life of spring how could this
happen?

We searched for signs; a feather from a striped
bird, or the fruit of the peach tree wearing the skin
of the elders. Who would lead us now? The voice
of reason was dead and still dying as we argued
into the next day.

Then the old woman spoke: A nightingale is only a
nightingale when it confesses its brightest colours
are hidden in its throat, and a dog becomes the
animal we know when it pulls love out of the
master's hand.

And as the mangled tree straightened a branch, our
tongues curled and no one spoke. And the silence
fell, and it fell like a man falling off a cliff without
having one moment to shout out his name, only the
silence filling his body, then the gorge, then the
lives of all who knew him. This was the travelling
silence, the twin of sorrow that knocks on every
door and never tires.

## After the Deluge

After the deluge water hammers surrendered. A
rainbow, washed out and white, hung in the
southern sky.

A bird tried to speak. No one wasted words. And
prayers that never wandered beyond the mouth
stood up reaching for their sound.

I heard the moaning of riverbeds and roots that had
been dragged away, and the strong arm of the
wind lifting the fragrance of frail colours in their
final hours.

After the deluge the kneeling, bowing and placing
of a cheek into the muck. And by the river, waves
sleeping with their heads on the shore.

Morning came with darkness and unsatisfactory
blue. We searched for food and I bit into a
childhood story savouring the salt that preserved
my youth.

The song of the earth rose from subterranean
gardens. Men buried their tears and danced the
dance of joy, all of us children, with clay on our
feet and innocence in our eyes.

## Autumn Knew No Mercy

Autumn knew no mercy. It encircled us from the east and the west forcing us to look at an angry sky.

The shoulders that once carried dreams sloped forward, and revenge crawled in the vineyards and abandoned gardens.

The words for 'sun,' 'breeze' and 'warmth' now covered in mud, trampled by the slow-moving feet of mules, and the cry from the deepest canyon was your own voice mourning a lost season.

Provisions were hoarded (winter always overstayed its welcome). The storytellers sharpening their tongues for the long nights ahead, carefully concealing words and snaring the warmth of summer.

Finally what one remembers is the same in every season: the fishermen lashing their prayers to the old boats, and the widows huddled together, counting whatever it was they counted.

And as the vision of the elder, asleep for so long, awoke in our hearts, we talked of burning the outer ring of fields, so the foot of disease would be cloaked in ash as it wandered nearby.

## Two Fingers of Sunlight

In the month of black heat our lungs refused the
air, the clouds pinned to the valley, and two
fingers of sunlight closed my eyes. And there I
was, in the near silence, building a hive for
yesterday's honey. My breath moved quickly
tying knots in the whispers and throwing the rope
further into someone else's ears. Then a cry from
the tree huts and a watchword fell like ripened
thunder. Everything stopped. I waited for the
moments to continue their long trek through the
desert, waited for the ocean to collapse its history
into one long wave, and listened as breastplates
and daggers rushed the shore.

## The Marauders

They came out of nowhere, from under a rock,
or the melody of the bluebird.

They came with white shadows in their eyes.

They came leaping over all the summers, and the
sighs of lovers.

They came with their daggers, in a bone-cracking night
carving the youth out of every man.

And lifting the weight of my fear I severed the
head of this day.

And in the fields a torn dress, hanging on the
naked branches, waiting for the girl who had
already begun her journey.

Yes, they came like the children running through
summer to this shallow place where everything
surrenders.

The lips tremble searching for that sound
the living cannot make.

# The Lone Survivor

When the ploughmen found him he was neither
dead nor alive.

The women in mourning took him in, tending
the wounds only they could see.

The warriors understood why he slept with an
axe, every night reconquering the same enemy.

His eyes always moving, searching through the
thickest part of hope, for those who would
somehow walk out of the mist.

After the harvest his pain spread to every
newborn thought, and he limped through his
days on a thin stump of darkness.

And when he hungered for this place that no
longer existed, he bit into all the laughter he had
known, and what some called a smile breached
his clenched lips.

More often a scream leapt over the trees and we
heard the cries of an animal refusing to die, not
from its wounds, but from a world it could see
and never touch.

## After the Harvest

After the harvest the fear of storm clouds floated
away. The besieged ponds and lily pads eyeing
their shadows. Another day weakened from the
weight of the sun resting on the river. In the
clearing, united under one banner, the battle with
weariness raged. No one stirred to tend the sick.
Love strayed into the unforgiving house of sleep,
the heart its own hand, bruised and calloused.
And the coarse words of the whalers' song
whispered like a lullaby, and nothing wakes you;
not the creaking door opening the dream or the
crowd of fears gathered around winter. And we
sailed on one thought: *May the river never open
its toothless mouth to flood the fields where I have
laboured.*

## The Cliff Dwellers

On their holy days they tossed handfuls of words
from the story of creation onto the plains, watering
them with whatever fell from their porous dreams.

They hungered for more than food, following
forbidden footprints, or marking a broken tree on a
cave wall, noting the broad shoulder of the wind.

And they said: In the cornfields yellow blessings, in
the sea a slave's song chained to the oar of one word,
and in the meadow the lost child below the weeds
stretching his voice into the melody of despair.

And when the night cuts the sky so that every
colour bleeds but does not die, this they called the
rainbow of darkness.

In the season of survival when the round beetle
retreats into its skeletal home and the floodwaters
chase the sea into the mountains, they blessed the
ancestral grounds with the untamed blood of a wild
animal.

They dug pits and holes in the earth to bury sorrow, a
barren season, or a frightful dream. And they asked the
dying to continue their journey over the ridge and onto
a cloud where the soul parted from the body,
remaining nearby.

## Sometimes

Sometimes the body of fog that rises over the
ponds is not a body. And sometimes you stare and
you stare as the lion's claw migrates into a goat's
tail or the beak of the eagle finally captures a
strand of deserted sky.

Sometimes it deceives us playing the drowned
man, sinking into the treasure of turquoise to
suddenly surface with fistfuls of laughter.

And sometimes I watch it drift away returning
home like the unwed maiden, lifting her white
gown to a whiter thigh, as she crosses the meadow
leaving her lover.

Sometimes it is the green banished from the
rainbow, bending over to soothe the anger of the
darkest of blue. And sometimes it is the calm of the
ocean pondering a wave.

Some say it's the palace guards running in their
savage red vests and tarnished shields with no
emblem except the word "Survive."

And sometimes the fog is the sound only the lilacs
know as they bend on their stems bracing for each
terrifying note.

Sometimes it is the long procession of the night
marching over its mountain path carrying the
weakest of grey and the carcass of a black elk
high on its shoulders.

Sometimes it's the forest in spring and then the
winter plains and a young fawn unaware of the
hunter, her bow and arrow, and then it is the tiny
hole in your heart and the angels' lullaby as we
fall headfirst and are suspended above our
thoughts in a shroud of mist over these ponds.

## Then I Enter the Sacred Grounds

I move away from the right side of indiscretion. I
move as if the walls are not there, as if the shadows
I am tired of wearing are tired of me. I see the
enemy's flag waving in front of me and I rejoice.
The moment I have feared is finally here. I turn to
glance at the unforgivable, to peer into the faceless,
deathless cage you wanted to build above the
mountain, where the vulture's obese eye barely
moves. I see the river floating over the side of the
wall, the anchor sinking into some past glory, and
then darkness, that exclamation point on the future
explodes. Later it will be hard to forgive the
silence, the harrowing sound of smoke, or to
handcuff the future with a word or two we owe to
the gods. There is little I can do. I memorize the
stories that were told to me in moans, harbouring
one mystery or another, and embrace the stone
shoulder where thousands of tears have come to
rest. Then I enter the sacred grounds, listen for the
hymnal of bees, and scatter my handful of thorns.
Knowing the deities are satisfied and man is hungry
brings me no relief.

## The Elder Tells the Story

There is a story I want to tell, a story many have
died trying to tell. It fell from the stone fortress
beyond the mountains, long before the famine fed
our mothers' fears and long after the seventh
shooting star had been counted.

This story is the childlike moment when silence
danced barefoot with silence and the river soothed
the hundred-year old ache in the back of the great
stone.

It is a fragment of the past that cut the eye of the
storyteller, the aftermath of some great eruption
whose tremors attached themselves to our beliefs
so we shake with fear and wonder as we walk.

If you listen the story is breathing and can be
heard as the night air whispers to the hawk and the
bird carries the secret in a beak that is plunged into
the neck of his prey. (This is the one way to bury
knowledge.)

And some have said it was the mother standing on
the edge of that shore, chasing her child's dream to
the place where the water was deepest and what
wanders to the surface, a hollow scream, the
realization that death was no longer wearing a
hunter's mask.

You must understand the story begins in a name
washed ashore that asks, "why play with the gods?"

Someone tries to light a candle, the wind will not
hear of it. Someone calls out to her lover and the
canyon erases the echo.

## In the Days of the Cotton Wind and the Sparrow

In the days of the cotton wind and the sparrow the
ponds refused to ripple. The memory of floods
carried us away and the sweet taste of water
stained our tongues. Some sought out caves,
others lay down in dugouts and covered
themselves with straw. And so it was with us. I
remember lying there with her, a bud of youth
spring had almost forgotten. We wandered into
the three forests of no return; the glance that sees
all, the smell that harnesses a fever to the blood,
and finally the first touch sealing one fate to
another. And although eternity was far away I
knew I would live forever in this moment.

## The River

There were secrets the river would never tell, like
how it bathed the stars or counted the shifting
clouds. This was the place where youth could
harness the white neck of fire and ride over all the
tomorrows.

And it was the holy mark lovers made on their
backs and across their chests that's never erased.
It was a promise swaying, a peasant who appeared
as a king and a king searching for the one soul he
could trust. And just as you reached out to touch it
saying, "I am here" – its muddy fingers broke off
in your hands.

The river told lies. It promised you dinner but
cradled its fish in the smallest of coves. The
storytellers understood this was where the past
was always changing. Seaweed was the long rope
that strangled a theory, and a pouch drifting to
shore altered one man's fate in the great story.

And the river refused to be sketched, altering its
appearance by pulling in a cheek, or turning its
face slightly to the east and submerging an
eyebrow. In the spring it was anger, in the winter
a chieftain whose final words "No compromise"
froze on the ruby handle of his sword.

And when it stood perfectly still it was the bell in a deserted town that forgot the sound of urgency. And those who knew say it was the shiver of lightning that lives in the spine of every fever, and at the same time a child asleep, unaware we were watching.

## On the Fifth Day

On the fifth day the wind whispered old names,
forbidden songs, and half-eaten memories grew
stale in our mouths. Lepers covered what
remained of their faces and the light scurried into
corners or lay face down in the tall grass. No one
tuned an instrument or cleared his throat.

Near the forest we joined hands in a circle and
waited for the rain that would cleanse us, or a
sound that would stir the emotions of the blood to
rise and run through fields where shadows never
wandered.

On the fifth day the old woman appeared. Those who
had seen death looked away, and drew lines in the air,
dividing an unseen world. Her hands massaged
music out of a goatskin drum and she whispered in a
language that was not our own. And the earth moved
as long-legged creatures and seahorses stranded in the
story of creation struggled for freedom.

On the fifth day stars broke their molds and light
fell out of the sky, and the bruised knee of night,
dark purple and streaks of yellow, struck our
faces. And we gathered ancient words without
ever calling them by name. There was nothing
anyone could say. A spear was thrown into the
heart of our mythology and we knew many were
wounded.

## In the Cave of Lost Souls

"There are moments that won't move on, mule moments that you kick or whip, before they lift a foot to test the fullness of the air. In a day of hardship, my friends, eternity can be found on earth."

And he leaned on his staff – a spyglass into the future – with symbols that had scratched their way out of his stories, curved lines we could not interpret, the tooth and claw of an animal we almost knew, (markings that had charmed the wood for years).

His warnings – quick and sharp – the very tip of the blade leaving a thin reminder. "Soon time will be disfigured, we'll find the morning sun in the evening sky and the night breeze stumbling through noon.

"Beware of the weight of glory, the mismanaged tale that spreads from one village to another and the expectations it leaves in its wake. Beware of turning your back on a prayer before the last word has ascended."

And as he rose the chatter began. It rang out in the open fields, wet its feet in the breakwaters and walked through the sand beds of lovers and into the communal places where it was severed into equal parts, one for every goddess.

And this is how I learned our history, one word at a time, how the wolf tongue salivates on tomorrow's prey, or turns gently to lick an old wound that healed so long ago.

# The Plowing Hand

And the stars burst and the heavens, some say,
refused to open.

In the window all is light, all is not forgiven.
Revenge reaches for a weapon, the sharpened
stone that knows only the smallest veins.

You wander down ancient steps to where your
siblings bathed and watch your thoughts sail in
the same waters. The river speaks in tongues to
ostracized petals, wind-ripped weeds and the red
fin that silvers the night.

And you plead for something other than what we
constructed from twigs and sharp words,
something other than the plowing hand sowing
vengeance into the land.

A stray traveller arrives at your door speaking a
different language and you understand what you
see; day-old hunger grooming the face of fear.

The moment contracts, the memory expands. The
remaining stars abandon their positions and leave
for home, or another sky.

And you see the couple who swallow the
forbidden egg, then turn blue and shining,
a thought wandering in the clouds.

## After the Battle

Somewhere in this enclave of loneliness, a
meadow and a corner of a meadow where nothing
is preserved except a childhood dream.

And now to stand before you like a raindrop on
the skin of your arm and to recount the tale of the
sky. Imagine the winter falling on you like a
shadow cutting off its tail or a blizzard arriving
without snow.

Failure is everywhere. It is the volcanic crease in
your stone face, an old song dividing a house
where the ash of sorrow lies; the thunder dropping
her head here or a satchel there, and the grass and
even the sun which no longer warms us.

You languish on the uneven road, strangle what is
already dead and then move forward, ignoring the
thoughts under your command. This is how
forgiveness eludes you.

Summon whatever is in the blood to battle and
refute the legends we were fed, not by closing our
mouths, or turning our backs, but by emancipating
the characters who walked so long ago, placing
them onto a new and fertile field.

And now to those who talk to themselves as if the
sky was an empty bridge, as if the memory of the
war blackened like a stake through the heart, as if
the teeth I am wearing are as borrowed as the
words I once spoke, as if the clouds miscalculating,
dive in low and we lie flat on our bellies, and the
anthill doesn't explode, doesn't render the season
obsolete.

And you, yes you, wanted something more from
these words, a map that would lead you further
astray, a youthful hand serving up answers to your
prayers, or to enlist joy to storm the fortress you
could never conquer with your own laughter.

I want to walk out into the open plains and sail, as
I once did, on clouds that were mine. But now we
are nomadic, chewing on the stale promise
of a winter resting ground, meandering through a
dream no longer ours. And so we arrive, always to
the same place, where we disperse the crowds of
anger by throwing stones at the ones we love.

## At the Desert's Open Door

The story began, as it always seems to without
warning. Suddenly wandering through the
bush or the plains, we begged for the fire,
cinnamon-laced flowers, a night palace staged
at the desert's open door, where every star was
accounted for, and the laughter that feeds
laughter.

On the other side of the woods the name-calling
– the red spruce shouting at the goldfinch –
and the wild grass demanding the stray hoof
of any beast flatten its tangled hair.

You imagine warmth, the victorious ray of
sunlight on the high ground above the hills,
and the skin of glass igniting the bones, the
downpour of sweat sweeter than honey.

Even in your sleep your thoughts are travelling
knee-deep in the sand. You wonder how long
it will take – this journey that leads you on –
how many stories will be severed from their
endless endings, and leave you to resurrect the
shards of a dream.

You start with what you know, the Noble Tent
– a place of worship; two watchtowers – the
steel eyes of the settlement, and then the
savage pit where more than one body lies.

In the coming months a silence, so green,
grows in the deepest canyons. Then and there
you witness the ancient rivalry – the silver
pincers surprising the sleeping darkness and
the malicious sound of the inconceivable that
refuses to leave your ears. And the black
feathers fall.

## The Keepers of the Fire

They coaxed the flame out of woodchips and bark,
or caressed the dark face of ash, turning it red with
anger.

At the seasonal celebrations they were the first to
arrive, decorating the firepits, removing the shame
from the felled trees.

They strung the gold wheat, a sun goddess' hair,
on dark branches, and waited for the flames to
pluck the sounds that pleased the celestial ear.

The elder with the long beard coddled the soft tips
of the flame when it was born, and later he tied a
green sash on its velvet waist and now he merely
whistles and those yellow legs leap in the fire.

We never questioned what they sprinkled on the
scorched earth or why they flayed the names of our
friends. We knew the calamity of a fire that refuses
to burn, the light smoke that kisses the wind with
its death song.

# The Naming of the Well

*for Jeff Bien*

*Who names the well? Anyone who has carried thirst.*

The summer well, that speaks to you in violet and
apricot, and the staggering well that falls on its
knees before you, breathless with its agony.

The emancipated well shouting "freedom" into
the whirling sands, and then closing its mouth,
forever.

The star-coloured well that sent you dreaming
when your tongue lashed its cool waters. And the
strangled well, filled with white venom.

The relentless well pursuing you through deserts,
villainous swamps and the long border of your
day.

The flamboyant well, with its cape of painful
colours, reminding you of stretched limbs and
burned skin.

And the prophetic well that tells you what you
already know; "tribes and herds will die from this
water."

The scar-faced well with her magnificent, impish eyes, that you now call naked blue.

The cursed well and the one that curses, the flying well that soars above you, its feathers softening the sun.

Well with the silk lips of the wind and the long black strands, that bored itself into your heart spring and filled with red waters.

The makeshift well that is a meeting place and a stone mouth.

The royal well, the fountain of forever within you.

All wells are childish playing with your image of taste and tongue, monastic, and overwhelmed, thinking of those outstretched hands.

The infant well that cannot speak the name of mother water. And the old well recounting how its streams were once sweet and now spittle between missing teeth.

The pious well, prostrate before you, praying for rain. And the salacious well that invites you in while the others are out in the fields.

The right-sided well and the left, tossing something down your throat, a twig, a granule of sand, or a misused word. And the middle well no one drank from, (or should I say trusted).

The coy well, some water some of the time.

The outcast well no one has seen for years.

And the ancient well, where one navigates the rope the way you would a great mystery.

In the underbrush and the bramble, a petal of a flower, lifeless, and sleeping, in the taste of late night visitors that somehow banished your thirst. You see this and ask, "How many days' walk, how many sunsets will come and go before the naming of the well?" And there is no answer, only a breeze that bruises your lips.

## First the Severing of the Head

First the severing of the head, then the long slit
from the throat to the belly. That's how the old
woman dissected a dream. Her staff pounded the
earth and brave men knew fear as she motioned the
dreamer closer.

Then the curved hand of silence covered our ears
and everything stopped; the long arm painting the
sky red, the churning of butter (which never stops),
and the wind, no longer breathing, waited with us.

She stood up, a shadow deceiving the darkness,
the widows sighed as handfuls of morning dew
woke us.

And spells leaked from her porous fingers as if they
were droplets of rain seeping through a crevice in
the Cave of Lost Souls.

A lone bird circled above us, the same bird that
cleansed these dreams, pecking at dark spots,
as if they were some ancient word we needed to
hear.

## Those Hills

Those hills were the anchors of inconsistency
moving at will through our dreams.

They were the three morning stars swaddled in
dew, the one bundle a stonecutter could not lift.

We kindled fire under their watchful eyes, and when
we approached them with the word 'mine' they
stood on their hind legs and we knew they'd never
be tamed.

Those hills were the colours of the seasons, the blue
knees of winter and the newly born thistle young
lovers pressed on the first nights of summer.

Robust, angular, the jaw of the miller and the
perpetual song of one bird or another. They never
moved, frozen, the five tears of youth behind the
eye of every elder.

Those hills challenged us, taught us the
incomprehensible laws of nature, and so we
climbed on their backs and rode the dusty names
of places travellers had never mentioned.

# The Wrath of Massure or How the Days Passed

We rode through the fog in the salting season.
Some claimed it was the wrath of Massure that
had followed us for years after eating the corn
before the harvest sacrifice, and we would never
see the ledges, too narrow for a horse or mule.

The days passed. I drew a perimeter around my
sanity, a wall against the white mirage of winter;
burning suns, complete warmth – men shedding
their clothes – and the deep lines in the hardened
earth revealed the thirst of every plant and grain
of sand.

Words were the sour taste of fruit when one
expected something sweet. We counted clouds,
trees, and the names of old enemies. This was the
way time was devoured.

Suddenly the relocated thought appears; the
unmade bed and the calibrated laughter that fit
perfectly into the moment. You remember the
first time you witnessed her lightning yellow hair
lighting the fire in your eyes, the unkempt sounds
that fell like those long strands.

A raven appeared on the fifth morning, so rare for
these parts, perched high above, as if painted onto
one stone. The water carrier claimed it wasn't real,
or was another bird disguised in a stray colour no
one had bothered to name. I ventured beyond words
glancing up, lifting my arms in an act of surrender
to whatever was there.

And those who had been ushered into the movement
of the quiet water sat by the shore, searching for
prayers that had not yet made it to the other side.

# Beyond the Borders of All I Know

Tonight the round shoulders of loneliness press
hard on the plow and the earth doesn't give
way.

How I envy the mist climbing at will among these
mountains, kissing the rock face, rising to some
heavenly place.

And tonight whoever paints the sky is tired. All I
see in the darkness is a string of silk, tarnished
feathers and the sharp green piercing the moon.

In the morning light less will be clear. The
falconer's glove forever hidden will attract the
same wave back to the shore.

And now to open the gate at the bottom of the
pond and swim to where water cherries blossom,
the thin lava breathing in golden fish, wandering
beyond the borders of all that I know.

I swallow the night air and remember the trip to
some forgotten place begins by cupping the
smallest of memories in your hands, and releasing
it, as you look away.

And then something so simple as the silver edge
of a falling leaf reminds me it is no more than one
pebble that seals us in the cave of our own sorrow.

# We Should Not Look into Each Other's Eyes

We should not look into each other's eyes.
There are wild horses, uncharted memories, and
the shadow that has followed us for too many
years.

Let us say, "yes" only when the moon is rising
and the river chasing a star. Let us say, "perhaps"
in the month of the monsoon when we can lengthen
our fears into the whip that lashes desire. And the
taste is never of blood.

And then it arrives, the hand of the uprising, and
the breath of fire that engulfs the ancient walls of
a history we were just making. You wanted the
glory of all conquerors, the parade, the pageantry
and rosebuds in your hair straying into magic. I was
searching for something too, as I emptied the
pockets of all of those dreams.

One evening swimming in the sands of a storm you
ruminated on the names of the sea. And there in the
cisterns when everyone removed their sandals, you
refused to even lift your skirt, whispering, "Submerge
yourself, drink only what is between the blue and the
green waters."

In the darkest corner of the night you were striking
light into an old myth we had carried. Some stopped
to listen, others scurried by saying it was bad luck
to let the ears touch these sounds.

And in the season of laughter when couples walked
into the low tide, you said, "Let me mark the
distances between love and its nomadic neighbour,
sorrow." And your feet barely moved.

In an outpost far from here you asked the watchmen
what they could see when they looked into the sky.
And they trembled as you decorated the hours,
flung banners over the minutes and held your
insignia high.

Now hunger is upon us, the snow is ripe but never
satisfying. The sorcerer it was said, once set fire to
the tree of knowledge after having eaten the belly of
its fruit. And I looked at you and wondered.

## Because

Because nothing is clear, not the mountain
streams the stars bathe in or the fruit in the coral
fields below the sea.

Because there are invincible seasons concealing
themselves in spring and fall, and I dreamt the
way lovers dream, with a smile on each of my
fingers.

Because there was no way to barge into the
crowded room and demand the ostrich feather that
was rightly mine, to end the rumour the river
spreads for a century, or silence the words that
were laid to rest in your home.

And because I languished here far too long,
because I sang as though my song was the first
and only song the valley would hear. Because in
that moment when all other moments die, the
rainbowed eye of the storm is smudged with
ashes and gathers lost children in the palm of its
hand.

Because the summertime is a frozen memory and you watch it thaw by the fire watering all that is fertile, because on the east embankment mud has claimed victory, because the wind-eaten grapes did not soothe the hunger of the storm gods and laughter was running away from us faster than death was approaching.

Because in the Black Forest everyone was waiting for the mellow evening star.

Because this is the time to execute the dying light, to demonize the tail feather of the peacock, and to murder the sword and the spear; to chain and unchain the heart to the same whipping post, and to feed pain and sorrow the same tortured memory.

Because somewhere in the marketplace, amid the squalor, the pigeons and the roosters with dreary coats, dreams were hatching. And the smiles of the young boys and girls made the same sound as bells in the farthest places.

Because the childish hand desires another form of magic, a small miracle, or an animated speech that is better than a tale.

Because the house of misery is never empty.

Because sandstorms come and go but to follow the footprints of the parables is a craft.

And because at a time like this to chronicle the world is to cast stones at a birthing mother.

## During the Summer Nights

During the summer nights the sky wore spurs that
kicked silver into the dark flanks of the moon.

This was the time of procrastination, slow
movements and slower thoughts.

The wind began its journey, carrying seedpods,
ancestral names, and the scent of wild flowers
infiltrated every dream.

In a sliver of light the vision of old men dancing,
fireflies and the long legs of crickets leading us
through the night.

We closed our eyes and the heat worshipped in the
tiniest of temples on the pilgrimage that follows
the veins into the heart.

In the late afternoon the sun harpooned shadows.
The light passed beyond borders, entered caverns,
estuaries, and went further, beyond the rage of the
father, lording his fields, and deeper into those
places where justice strangles compassion.

## I Am Still Here (A Goddess Speaks from the Mouth of a Man)

I am still here in the green, and the red of the wild
haze, and the aftermath of a story I never wrote. My
greedy fists clutch at your skin and the hereafter.

I am an old saying that lost its meaning on the stone
steps of an indifferent century, a name banished but
still humming. I was the decree written for your
enemy that followed you home, a string of "goodbyes"
uttered to no one but the tall grass and the sad, sad
song I invented at my birth.

And you want to turn away, you want to turn back
to touch your youth or bathe in the warmth of a
summer day. You plead with the delinquent star to
shine, or watch the severed hand of a great warrior
as it appears in the sky. Then a fist, yellow knuckles
and a storm strikes the earth. And nothing can stop
the rains.

That is why I am here, in the condemned corner of
this song, in the sweet bread and the cornmeal your
hunger ignores. I am the assassin of good news,
reaching for one more quiver of darkness, and the
moon draping the sky with a sideways kiss.

A flock of geese flutters over the pond, cleaving
the fragrance of the night, and what is slender fits
into the palm of my hand; the cold light and the
immobilized thought, and I am what some call
deep water, the blackened forest, danger by all its
names.

Let me stop here, beyond these hills to view what
has kept me alive, the retreating breeze that always
caressed my cheek, the pink encroaching on red
petals and that interloper purple, leaning on the spell
I cast on summer.

And I am the one who commanded insects to build a
better life and tall trees to squander their chances of
touching the clouds.

If I stumble, fall face down, and disappear in the
dust, remember my left hand in a fatal attempt to
lasso the lone figure wandering through the
calligraphy on the cave wall, the word before it
was pronounced hollow.

# The Seasons Changed

The great indecision, the wanderings and the
return.

The outlook that is bleak and still alive is
something strange like the fragrance of spring
in mid-winter, or the boats that returned and
those that did not.

The seasons changed and nothing grew in this
country like boredom. We listened to the
thunder rehearsing in its squalid home.

And the rhythmic chains of slaves, pulling
together as the first blossom was lifted out of
the earth.

The leaves had fallen. A traditional song
played on a hollowed-out piece of wood. Later
we learned it was only the wind blessing the
streams with blossoms, whiter than pure
thought, and the underground swell capturing
our feet.

We moved on in silence. Out here reminiscing
could kill a man. We were all painting the
same picture of agony, though the colours
differed. No one expected to see the shooting
pain of yellow in the twisted limb, the swath
of red in the silhouette of the women weeping,
or the golden tip of a black tooth burrowing
into a lifeless jaw.

Monotony was the forest, the stream and the
plains. The names of days vanished. The hours,
shackled, shuffled by. Was this the moment in
between, when time stumbled and lost count
of its soft footfalls?

We looked to the mountains where mercy was
buried in the crevices, the miracle still
undecided if today would be the day.

## Second Dream

In the dream the rich colours of the season cover
me. I surrender my home and the river extends its
hand just as my own recedes. Longing is
everywhere. The dream is never just a dream. We
dissect it slowly, lifting the skin of the heart before
the wings flutter and it flies to who knows where.
We try to unravel the message coiled on the severed
foot left behind or pry open the beak where a word
is marooned. The story begins, the river rises, the
rebellion at dawn and later the sky that surrenders its
name for blue. The wind chimes waiting with the
bells and the flowers rehearsing how their petals will
fall. The storm clouds break. And nothing wakes me,
not the chorus at the tip of the sword of ecstasy, or
the weight of a leaf landing on my forehead. Then
it came: the rain that drowns sheep and muzzles
men, a century of rain falling from the eye of one
warrior. You see, the half moon is the cradle for the
unconscious that leaves you rocking between "The
world I've seen" and "The world I know."

## And So in the Fifth Year

And so it was in the fifth year of vengeance, the
fifth year of reluctance to take a vow, and the fifth
year of the famine that never ended, I came to this
place.

You see in the tiniest of gardens and in the rivers
that felled rainbows, I entered a shadow that
wasn't mine and wandered away from time. I
remember the eclipse, the encounter with the holy
and the ripened sound of joy that greeted me. And
how I danced with the earthly vibrations and a bell
tolled.

A voice called out, "Never forget what you cannot
hear: the sound of healing; the web fermenting in
the open wound, or the curse of a goodness that
sweeps us over the edge of our understanding."

Then the cry at midnight and the thunder yawning,
tired of all this darkness and gloom. The rain fell
and the stiff feet of winter barely moved on the
road to spring.

And all my dreams taverned in this crowded
place, staggered through the door. And slowly I
relinquished the fear I held, nurtured and yes,
loved.

## The Travellers

They came with news of lush fields and great altars,
that had been only a whisper, a hint of a spice
barely touching the tongue.

In some faraway place they learned the customs for
greeting sorrow, how the body should be turned just
so and the head tilted to the right, avoiding its full
embrace.

And they knew how to measure the arch of sunlight,
to calculate the warmth of the waters, and
understood when to become a tree in the forest, or
lie flat on the earth listening to the approaching
dangers.

We watched the way words turned in their palms
and stood like piles of stone on the plains, marking
a great feat that should be acknowledged by a
passerby (even if the details were unknown).

And they came with the laughter of drowning men
who went mad watching the yellow-tailed fish and
the thoughts that were the final breath of their fate.

They spoke as one speaks when making a solemn promise, they spoke the way trackers do on the sixth day of searching for a well. And when disdain covered their faces we knew the taste of brackish water.

## Listen to Me Like You Have Listened to the Rain

Listen to me like you have listened to the rain, its
short and long fingertips tapping out a melody
you cannot ignore.

The dull day, the sound of thunder that lightning
refuses to follow.

In the far-off reaches the light is courting a
shadow. Shyly it moves in, stretches out an arm,
and places an ochre hand around a slim vibration
or the waif of a flower.

You shield your eyes. There is no blood, no
ferocious saying lying at your feet, no divine
image of the wandering one, no avoiding the
drumming of the cognitive, those fugitive
thoughts, the bequested, the almost suffering and
never ending.

Then the pure white or black, the shoulder that
invents a head, the sorrow that builds half a bridge
from here to the middle of who-knows-where, and
that little thing appears, barely a tic, a dryness in
the mouth that spreads to your skin, and doubt
announces itself.

And you observe it all, answering to names no one
has ever called you; tyrant, king, miser, miserable
one, and the orchids bloom, the child sings, and
someone throws a curse that strikes your ear.

Yes, the days were divided. Some went north
others south, dusk mingling with dawn, crimson
and blood-red, laughter and more laughter,
madness conjugating sanity.

And far away in a corner of the garden, where the
lilacs have been refused entry, where the seeds
were planted and in yesterday's hours trimmed,
the dream was flowering, calling me a name I did
not know, a name I would remember.

# Those Who Knew the Healing Herbs

They were river captains entering an unmarked
bay, coaxing illness to the left and slightly to the
right, avoiding the heart, liver or lungs.

They knew their way through the back door of
disease, entering with their torches and flaming
words that burned the gates of those forgotten
cities where death's nomadic groan wandered.

And they settled on the great battlefield where
the relentless wave clawed stubborn mountains,
and the soft sound of stones, barely alive,
rippled in their ears.

And what surrounded them frightened us: the
crane's neck, the setting sun drifting on the beak
of a raven, and the dark face of a figure we
never knew.

They studied the thin veil of the wind and
listened to the tremors that barely spoke under
the skin.

Mostly they bottled the sparks from fireflies, the silver threads from spray-fish or anything that could bring light to a dying man's eyes and lead him back to his birth story. This was all any of us could hope for.

## In the Freezing Waters

In the freezing waters no one remembers his name
or the village where he was born.

In tiny pockets of resistance the flesh fighting for
the memory of warmth. And in the sphere beyond
all spheres, the seeds of green planting water on the
tongue.

Eyes heavenward, the turquoise in the skyline ties
your thoughts to the tentacles of the sea.

The future a succulent fruit, stranded on the
branches above you.

Tossing the heaviest of vows, crying out the names
of all the gods, even those that must never be named
or touched by the lips.

A blue star crosses over the meadow where
seahorses roam. Your story now chained to the
moment that reveals the slender hand of the lunar
pull and the indiscretions of a summer sky. This is
how the wave opens its arms to embrace you.

## The Retelling of One Truth

I travelled through the mist as if I was the
sea-leopard, spotted and unseen, in the algae
and the green. This is the story of survival in a
place where everyone thrived. This is about
the threat of summer when the hunt was going
so well.

Perhaps this is the insomniac's dream, where
wide-eyed you are preparing for the feast and
the slaughter at the same time. This is difficult,
but you have trained yourself to cook what you
believe will be in your hands, and if nothing
appears secretly devour what you have
imagined.

There is a truth I want to retell and I see words
barely breathing below the surface. I grope and
still only empty hands. And so in these barren
lands I search for something else like a purple
stone that can describe joy, or the melody that
skips and strays into every thought carrying
the sharp memories that slice open laughter.

Look, they said evil was approaching from all
sides. Those who knew deciphered the stray
boulders that had found their way onto our path
and a crushed plaster god of light smouldering.

Silver polished the tip of its spear with the
moss, the spine of darkness stiffened, and
feathers were fanning more than the flaming
colours pitched in red. The foot of a giant was
born and you watched the grass and trees bend,
the old remedies thicken. Without warning the
grasshoppers ended their century-long vigil.
Silence inched forward. And those with an eye
to the future were salting history with
mischievous hands.

## In the Nights When Nothing Was Sacred

In the nights when nothing was sacred, the songs
were all we had. We dipped words in the voices of
those who had passed this way: the grey-haired
seer who pulled the moon's blessings one ray at a
time into her eyes and onto the people. And the
old one with the knotted fingers who suffocated
storm clouds by pressing her palms together.
Their voices skipped over the mountains, and the
valley refused to swallow the echo. A young girl
dressed in white escaping the borders of flesh and
bone, floated to the centre of the circle. We
listened to her feet that almost danced, arrows
striking the many hearts of silence, and were
soothed by the rhythmic tapping – that was the
heartbeat of the earth.

## The Quiet of Stones

Then the quiet of stones
and a fallen leaf
slicing the tip of my knowledge
and there are scattered images
a frail history that no longer speaks
and the smell of ashes travelling on.

# I Remember the Days

I remember the days when lightning illuminated
nothing more than fear. How the elder's laughter
migrated into the valley and the stars arched into a
bridge where we travelled.

You could hear the heavy footsteps in the woods,
and noted the way the red leaves surrendered. The
sleeping hunters, their amulets tucked in the
wheatgrass, and blessed by the unseen that taps a
head, an arm or thigh.

The clouds scratched out orange or yellow lines,
and green, a lonely victim, drowning in the first
wave of darkness.

Those whitewashed days of my youth, covered
over with monotonous chores, and the red days
that provoked blood are somewhere still bleeding.

Once in the height of battle with the smoke
reaching into our eyes, and the death rattle clearly
in our thoughts, I heard a man talking calmly,
rocking himself in the four words that birth gifts
each of us.

We listened for the hooves stuttering over the
plains, the days of awe approaching, not on a
white steed but on a tired packhorse, dry-mouthed
and hungered.

The first person to hear the trickle of a stream
cried out to the wilderness so that the naked
trees, the hibernating pollens and seeds, and the
night-blue stones, the soft shale we slept on,
would know the eternal sound of joy.

# No One Will Forget

No one will forget how the hand of sorrow fell on
our backs, how the shy river reluctantly
approached the shore, how we wished for an
elongated saying that would serve us well, a
washed-up prayer that still fits into the ear of the
gods, or a new remedy that would deceive a fever
into knocking on our neighbour's door.

Because on that morning people began
straightening the colours of their lives: crimson
for happiness, tortoise blue for solitude, and
sapphire for something else I've already forgotten.

Long ago there were rumours and indiscretions
that the underworld almost forgave. Once the tiny
differences could leap one to another, and the
sound of thunder was not a call to prayer.

And what bled wasn't wine-coloured water or the
darkness of tears but a reminder of the downpour
of splendour.

And now to grow the wheat that will strip the
names of everyone I know bare so that I will see a
person and call them what they really are: "brave,"
"evil," "misunderstood."

Somewhere else a story was being built, a vast
legacy, an angry myth climbing the midnight vine.

And somewhere the secret oath was given, a flock
of birds abandoned the trees, our footprints stalled
in their tracks. The anvil landed on the mallet
shattering injustice, reliving a dream that was
once a homeland.

## It Was the Time Before

It was the time before the spoken word, when the
wind was searching for its voice and spit nettles
onto the earth. A time when the shell competed
with the stone to see who would encase the egg,
and the stiff spine of the river had not eyed the
serpent's body. And angels who never argued
were discussing white or blue.

It was that time when the seas, swollen and
disfigured, floated in the deadest part of the sky,
when the thresholds of pain and hunger were still
undiscovered inlets, and the taste of pleasure was
about to be sweetened.

And it was the time of disenchanted boulders
pounding on the plains and a time of courageous
endeavours when green plants stood against a
southern wind, and the feathers of the peacock
searched for colour.

Cravings and desire met on the mountainside
lighting the torches that would set the blood on
fire. And the stillborn thunder buried its head in a
cloud.

Yes, this was the time of misplaced understandings
and impoverished wine, that slender season that
slips in between spring and the first fruit fall. A
time of shepherding the lilacs into a brighter
yellow.

And high above on the ramparts the night
watchman swung a silver chain cutting the throat
of the beast that devoured the light, and beyond the
moon's locked gate a goddess dancing, her twisted
feet stirring the clouds.

I swear it was the moment when waves walked on
the shore, before the slaying of the northern star
and the hanging of that bright carcass in the heavens.

It was the time of the grey cane prodding dark
green meadows westward in the sky, a time of
rumblings and confusion that breached the
immeasurable silence, the messenger remaking
the garden.

## In the Prevailing Light

It is here in the prevailing light, and in the
moment that leans on the future as it sinks into the
shadows, always the shadows, searching for its
place of rest, that I will reveal the secrets that
slept so silently within me.

I want you, more than anyone else, to know this –
the dark stick the night uses to beat the sky is only
a twig with aspirations, a shade of emptiness,
only a farewell to the oasis of a dream you nursed
for so many years.

Remember how you placed those little drops of
hope inside her opened mouth and rested in that
breath of jasmine and sage, the royal breath that
weaves you into the heavens.

And what is riveted to your tongue – the taste of
the feudal wars – will escape your memory, silence
the gold lines that crept into your face, and bow to
a new paradise and an old way of reaching it.

I want to call on all that is good, and all that is
evil, to patrol the outer ridge of our camp, and to
march over the Hill of Tears into the voice of
sorrow.

The river swims by itself and knows loneliness,
and courage is off wandering. Do not ask when
will it return. Here the fallen are childish notions
you cherish and so bending to your knees weep.
Prepare to resurrect yourself with a new purpose,
a better purpose, a forgiving hand.

## One Day

One day a sad song was climbing the fig tree for
no other reason than to look down on you. The
moon told the sun it would be late and we
watched the crimson speech, the purple finger
pointing and the long arm shaking in the sky.

The clouds cast dark smiles on the mountain paths
and we turned to the mysteries almost in our grasp
that scurried into the wilderness, and all that we
saw was the wisp of a white tail, or the river
turning black, conceding that the melody of a
certain bird is brighter than its finest blue.

And now to move further into the rainbow, to
pluck the feathers from the arrow so that death is
not a colourful assassin. And then the armies
marching, the conquerors, the feudal impositions,
the boundaries between the sunset and the sun,
blurred.

We enter the forest of Stray Crows reciting an
oath taken long ago. The warrior drops his sword,
the old rooster sleeps all morning, and we search
for that moment where the solemn light promises
tomorrow.

And then nothing, not the quartering of shame,
not the ground opening its wounds to show us its
broken ribs and the marvellous swelling on the
outer ridge of its thigh.

Only the starlight building a home far from here,
far from the rusting chimes and the paralyzed
sounds, reaching for a way out of time.

## The River that Must Be Crossed at Midnight

And so the nightfall and the falling rain, the
apparition of the wandering minstrel leaping
from the height of his last note. Then there is
the thunder, that ancient cry of anguish.

It's true I buried an old secret in your side.
The south wind was calling and I imagined a
caravan of jewels, your long hair and a white
steed under a full moon. Instead there was a
tired grey mare on the darkest of nights when
even the stars wore morning black.

In the clearing a bird saluted you, dipping one
wing. A terrified tale welcomed you by ripping
a branch from a tree as if it were an arm of a
man.

And there in a makeshift camp in the
mountains, ignoring the wounded, you
consoled those who looked far away, saying
"Now the healing can begin."

Someone said, "She is a crumb of an old
wives' tale devoured over the years, and still
men salivate over such a small thing."

Look the tide was rushing in, no one disputes
that. It was the way your webbed hand slapped
the waves that made people suspicious, and
for those waiting to witness something, you
were the leathery hide one chews and chews
and never swallows.

Somewhere else the sea is blessing a blue
stone, cattle are grazing and clouds forming.
And then the river that must be crossed at
midnight beneath a falling star, and a field that
is never where it once seemed to be.

## I Was Told They Would Return

I was told they would return. That their stay
would be short, and when the days were stretched
out and the light covered most of the night, we
would see their faces.

I was told to prepare the firepits and peel back the
skin of a wasting hour, to wait by the canyon for a
sign only I would know.

To listen for the echo from the battle of creation,
that squelched sound when the first webbed foot
touched a small island.

I was told to unravel the sacred cloth, to bury the
words I once knew and to place a lapis stone in
front of the blank eye of the elder. This was the
only way to search out the boy lost inside the old
man.

Nothing was wrapped in leaves or torn from the
breast of its mother, nothing stood tall or asked
for forgiveness. No shade of grey was driven out
of its home or bled into a cloud-white sky. No
answer was given to the weary, and "how long"
and "why" wandered hand-in-hand along the
banks of a starlit river.

The vibrations shook the branches of trees, the warring councils dividing the spoils below the earth, the face paint the gods wear before wedding a barren field to a fruitful season.

The moment was approaching, the quilt makers threading thick rope, long irons forged in the earth's belly. In the midst of all this – the thirst for the unknown, and the reverence for whoever pulls the seasons or the seas – I remembered the warnings of the river dwellers and how fools stumble over holy treasures and I closed my eyes, recounting everything I was told.

## Acknowledgements

My thanks to:

Barry Callaghan for his kindness and belief in this collection of poetry, and for the long conversation on those subjects we gravitate to: Russia and Russian poets, Amichai, the Blues and the C harp.

Michael Callaghan, for having published and designed the book, and for the time he invested in this project.

Jeff Bien, my brother, who waited at the border for these poems to arrive, and helped lead them through a literary labyrinth, offering them music and magic, so they could take their place in the world.

A.F. Moritz, who read multiple versions of the poems and the manuscript, on far too many occasions, and provided valuable suggestions.

Don Domanski, who worked on this book with me in its early stages through the Wired Writing Program at the Banff Centre for the Arts.

*The New Quarterly* (*TNQ*) and its editor Pamela Mulloy for publishing numerous poems from this collection over the years and for nominating "The Naming of the Well" along with two of my other poems, for the 2014 National Magazine Award for Poetry.

The editors of *Vallum Magazine* and *ELQ/Exile: The Literary Quarterly*, where poems in this collection first appeared.

The 2011 Montreal International Poetry Competition, and its judges, for selecting my poem, "They Escaped in the Night" as a finalist in its contest, and publishing it in *The Global Poetry Anthology* (Vehicule Press, 2012).

The Canada Council for the Arts, the Ontario Arts Council (OAC), and the Banff Centre for the Arts, for grants and scholarships; and the following literary magazines and publishers who recommended these poems for OAC Writers Reserve Grants: Brick Books, *Descant*, Guernica Editions, and *The New Quarterly*.

Paul Hamann, for an in depth interview he conducted with me on my writing for *The New Quarterly* (Fall 2013).

Michelle, Eli, Natacha, and my entire mishpucha, who stood with me when it mattered most.